Magic Ritual Baths
a guide to spiritual bathing techniques

© Alexis Morrigan

Copyright © 2012 by Alexis Morrigan
All rights reserved. No part of this publication may be reproduced, distributed, or transmitted in any form or by any means, including photocopying, recording, or other electronic or mechanical methods, without the prior written permission of the publisher, except in the case of brief quotations embodied in critical reviews and certain other noncommercial uses permitted by copyright law.
First Printing, 2012

When and How to Take Your Ritual Bath

Your Bathtub	7
Timing of Ritual Baths	8
Days of the Week	9
Phases of the Moon	11
Creating Your Own Ritual Bath	12
Color Correspondences	13

Ritual Baths

Power Baths

Psychic Energy Bath	16
Psychic Power Bath	17
Psychic Power Bath #2	18
Aura Energy Bath	19
Energizing Bath	20

Healing Baths

General Healing Bath	21
Emotional Healing Bath	22
Healing a Cold Bath	23
Anti-Depression Bath	24

Peace Baths

Peace Bath   25

Elemental Baths

Air Elemental Bath   26
Water Elemental Bath   27
Earth Elemental Bath   28
Fire Elemental Bath   29

Money Baths

General Wealth Attraction   30
To Attract Family Wealth   31
Attract Money for a Specific Purpose   33
Getting a Job   34
Financial Turn it Around Bath   35
Prize Winning Money Bath   36
Debt Banishing Bath   37
Good Business Bath   38
Business Bath for a Specific Need   39

Love Baths

Couple's Bath   40
Third Date Bath   41
Looking for Love   42
Increase Sexual Energy   43
Strengthen a Romantic Relationship   44

Romantic Dreams Bath	46
Romantic Attraction Bath for Men	47
Romantic Attraction Bath for Women	48
Have Faith Bath	49
Add a Spark to Love Bath	50
Special Occasion Romance	51
Love Drawing Bath	52
Beautiful Body Bath	53

Banishing Baths

Banish Negativity	54
Banish Soreness	55
Banish Anxiety	56
Banish Sadness	57
Banish Anything	58

Protection Baths

Uncrossing Bath	59
Uncross Thoughts	60
Uncrossing any Hex	61
Curse Removal Bath	62
Uncross Evil	63
Uncross Negative Energy	64

Luck Baths

Basic Luck Bath	65
Good Luck While Travelling	67

Healthy and Wealthy with Luck	69
Lucky Winner	70
Daily Luck Ritual	71

Your Bathtub

There are a few things to consider before beginning a ritual bath. First, you should have the right ambiance. Your home and especially the bathroom should be cleared of distractions and other people if at all possible. Most especially, your bathtub should be sparkling clean. If you are unable to get some time where you know you won't be bothered, or you are unable to perform your ritual with a clean tub, it is probably best put off for another night. By starting with the right environment, you will improve and enhance your chance of success.

Most ritual baths will instruct you to use something in the water that you would probably prefer not to go down your drain. There are a few ways to handle this. You can always place everything directly in the water. Once finished with your bath, you can use a net to retrieve everything. This is the least desirable option. You can also use a drain trap, which is a form fitting screen that is placed over your drain temporarily, and will catch any debris so it can be easily removed when your ritual is complete. This would be better than the first option.

What you should most likely do is hang a cloth bag over the faucet which you will then place herbs in. The water will run through it, infusing the herbs in your bath. This will make for the simplest clean up when your bath is over, and the cloth bag can be tossed in your washer. You could also make a cloth bag by hand, or even several, in different colors, to be used with corresponding ritual baths. If you don't have access to a bathtub but would still like to have a ritual bath, you can tie a cloth bag over your shower head to achieve the same effect.

Timing of Ritual Baths

Your first consideration in timing should be whether or not *you* have the time. If you are going to have to rush through your ritual bath, or if there is going to be a person waiting on you, put your bath off for another day. When you take your bath, you should have the time to go through it properly for the greatest chance of success.

Secondly, you can take into consideration what day of the week it is, and what phase the moon is, and how that corresponds to the ritual you want to do. Your ritual work will always be greater if you pair the right ritual with the right time.

Days of the Week

Sunday

Colors: Yellow, orange, or gold
Deities: Sun
Element: Fire
Spells: Beauty, friendship, healing, creativity, authority, achievement, success, and goals

Monday

Colors: Silver or white
Deities: Moon
Element: Water
Spells: Home and family life, healing, intuition, and growth

Tuesday

Colors: Red or orange
Deities: Mars
Element: Fire
Spells: Courage, intellect, strength, discipline, enemies, and conflict

Wednesday

Colors: Purple
Deities: Mercury
Element: Earth
Spells: Career, communication, travel, finance, intelligence, legal matters, and general luck

Thursday

Colors: Green or royal blue
Deities: Jupiter
Element: Fire
Spells: Honor, family, loyalty, faithfulness, and prosperity

Friday

Colors: Pink or aqua
Deities: Venus
Element: Air
Spells: Love, romance, fertility, luxury, art, harmony

Saturday

Colors: Black or dark purple
Deities: Saturn
Element: Earth
Spells: Creativity, hope, change, and removes negativity

Phases of the Moon

New Moon

New beginnings, transformations, health, love, romance and hope

Waxing Moon

Accomplishments, growth, success, health, creativity, and learning

Full Moon

Manifesting, sexuality, protection, legal work, finances, and achievements

Waning Moon

Cleansing, releasing, banishing, ending

Dark Moon

Resting and peace

Creating Your Own Ritual Bath

You can also always create your own, or add to ritual bath instructions you are following. This is very simple to do and you can plan in the basics of your bath, or what you would like to add to a bath you are reading about, in just a few minutes.

Start with a basic recipe for bath salts. This is simply a half cup of Epsom salts, a teaspoon of sea salt, 15 drops of the essential oil you feel corresponds correctly with the ritual bath you would like to have, and optionally, 5 drops of food coloring in the appropriate color for your work. Combine these ingredients together and there you have it, customized bath salts that meet your needs exactly.

You can continue with your planning by picking between 3 and 5 dried herbs which accentuate your intentions, and a candle in the appropriate color. Other things you could incorporate include crystals, or maybe a chant or prayer. Gather your supplies and your willpower and you are on your way to a successful ritual bath.

Color Correspondences

White

White represents balance and is the lunar color. It can be substituted for any other color. It represents cleansing, clairvoyance, healing, and enlightenment.

Silver

Silver represents the moon Goddess, reincarnation, the removal of negative energy, stability, and intuition.

Red

Red represents Aries and Scorpio, love, health, passion, fertility, willpower, strength, courage, sexuality, determination, and increases magnetism in spell work.

Pink

Pink represents love, fertility, romance, femininity, friendship, emotional love, healing, peace, and honor.

Magenta

Magenta is used to hasten results.

Orange

Orange is a solar color and represents Leo, creativity, confidence, ambition, legal or business success, kindness, encouragement, and good luck.

Yellow

Yellow is a solar color and represents vitality, change, progress, safe travel, an increase in learning abilities and mental prowess, energy, and also helps with visualization and the creative process.

Gold

Gold represents the sun deities, solar energy, general financial success, success with investments, world power, luxury, will increase your ability to overcome obstacles, and can attract cosmic energy.

Green

Green represents the Goddess, money, prosperity, wealth, nature, fertility, animals, peace and peace in your home.

Blue

Blue represents sea or sky deities, truth, wisdom, bravery, courage, calmness, honor, harmony, and can cause prophetic dreams to increase or become clear.

Purple

Purple represents Saturn and the elements, counteracts negativity and black magic, reverses curses, and increases psychic and meditative power.

Brown

Brown represents the earth and earthly beings, material increase, and attracts lost objects.

Gray

Gray is used to cancel out negativity, and for complex meditation and visualization.

Black

Black represents the deities of the underworld and Saturn. It is used to repel or to banish negativity, and to free yourself of bad habits.

Psychic Energy Bath

This bath may be taken before casting spells or attempting divination.

Handful of fresh thyme
Sprig of patchouli
½ cup dried yarrow
Petals of a white rose
Whole nutmeg
Lukewarm bathwater

Add the thyme, patchouli, yarrow, and nutmeg. The rose petals should be added last.

Enter the bath and relax with closed eyes. Bring about peace of mind and welcome calmness into your body. Remain in the water at least 15 minutes, or until you feel relaxed and that your innate psychic abilities are at their peak.

Psychic Power Bath

This bath is intended to increase your psychic abilities.

1 cup fresh lemongrass
¾ cup fresh thyme
Ground orange rind, it is also best you have eaten the orange
Cinnamon stick
5 whole cloves
Very hot bathwater

Add the lemongrass, thyme, orange rind, cinnamon stick and cloves.

Allow the bath to cool to an appropriate temperature before submerging yourself. Meditate for at least 20 minutes, focusing on your relaxing your mind, and opening your mind up to the unseen and unknown.

Psychic Power Bath #2

This bath is intended to increase your psychic abilities.

1 cup dried yarrow
½ cup dried bay leaves
Very hot bathwater

Add the yarrow and bay leaves.

Allow the bath to cool to an appropriate temperature, and stir the water with your dominant hand before submerging yourself. Meditate for at least 20 minutes. Focus on being totally at peace with yourself. You may visualize your mind reaching outwards, searching for general or specific knowledge.

Aura Energy Bath

This bath is intended to strengthen and rejuvenate your aura.

3 sprigs thyme
3 sprigs marjoram
Lukewarm bathwater

Add the thyme and marjoram.

Submerge yourself and remain in the bath for at least 15 minutes. Visualize yourself and your aura as you see it currently. Once you have a good picture of your aura, focus on increasing it, changing its color, or just focus on its inner strength.

Energizing Bath

This bath is intended to increase your personal energy.

Petals of 3 pink carnations
Sprig of rosemary
Sprig of basil
Handful of lavender flowers
Very hot bathwater

Add the carnation petals, rosemary, basil, and lavender flowers to steaming bath water. As temperature allows, stir the water clockwise with your dominant hand.

Submerge yourself in this bath and focus on becoming calm and relaxed. Slowly begin to visualize yourself as filling up with energy. With each inhale, you take on energy. With each exhale, you let go of any inhibitors or negativity. Continue breathing in energy for at least 10 minutes, or as long as it takes you to feel completely energized.

General Healing Bath

This bath is intended to increase your general health.

Ounce of dried mint leaves
Ounce of dried chamomile
Cup of Epsom salt
Blue washcloth
Hot bathwater

Add the mint leaves, chamomile, and Epsom salts.

Submerge yourself and carefully wash your entire body, starting at your head and moving down towards your feet, with the blue washcloth. As you are washing yourself, visualize your body as whole and healthy.

Soak for at least 30 minutes while visualizing your body in perfect health, with a white light of protection surrounding you. Start by seeing the white light right in front of your eyes, and expand it so that it covers your neck, your chest, each arm, your torso, and eventually covers your feet.

Emotional Healing Bath

This bath is intended to heal emotional pain and anguish.

7 drops violet oil
7 drops camphor oil
7 drops hyssop oil
Purple candle
Your preferred temperature bathwater

Submerge yourself. Drop by drop add violet, camphor, and hyssop oil.

Light the purple candle and place it in a corner of the bathtub near your feet, you should be able to see the flame while lying back.

Submerge yourself and soak in the tub for at least 10 minutes. Empty your mind of stress and worry and imagine you are in perfect emotional and physical health.

You shouldn't exit the bath until your mind is calm and relaxed. Once you are ready to exit, drain the water and watch it drain. As the water is going down the drain, know that it is taking with it your emotional distress.

This bath should be repeated for 7 consecutive days to help heal emotional distress.

Healing a Cold Bath

This bath is intended to heal your common cold.

3 ounces white vinegar
Petals of 3 purple pansies
10 drops camphor oil
Very hot bathwater

Fill the bathtub halfway with very hot water and add the pansy petals and camphor oil. Add the vinegar and stir the water with your dominant hand as temperature allows. Then continue filling the tub.

Submerge and soak yourself for at least 15 minutes, taking deep breaths and remaining as still as possible.

Continue to take this bath each day until you feel completely well.

Anti-Depression Bath

This bath is intended to ward off depression.

Whole lemon, halved
Whole orange, halved
Handful of chamomile
Handful of lavender
Handful of marjoram
Lavender or apple scented soap
Your preferred temperature bathwater

All ingredients should be as fresh as possible. Add the lemon and orange halves, chamomile, lavender, and marjoram to hot running water. Then continue to run the water as you normally would.

When the tub is full, submerge yourself. Take several deep breaths, keeping your eyes open. Scrub your entire body, starting at the top of your head and working down to your toes with the soap. Adding more hot water is okay, it is important to be warm and comfortable during this bath.

Meditate in the water, taking slow inhales and exhales, for at least 10 minutes. This bath may be repeated as often as necessary to ward off depression.

Peace Bath

This bath is intended to promote peace and decrease anxiety.

Handful of dried lavender
Handful of dried chamomile
Handful of dried linden
Pot of water
Warm bathwater

Add herbs to the pot of water and place it where the sun will shine on it throughout the day. At nightfall, strain the mixture into a warm bath.

Submerge yourself and remain in the water for at least 20 minutes. Whatever you are worried about or anxious over, this is the time to address it. Think of each worry. If the worry isn't very specific, make it so. Form a complete sentence for your one worry. Once you have the worry specified, gently push it out of your mind. Continue to do this with each of your worries, one at a time until you have addressed each worry.

When you are finished with the bath, watch the water as it drains. Visualize each worry spinning down the drain with the water.

This bath can be repeated weekly.

Air Elemental Bath

This bath is intended to promote change.

3 tablespoons lavender
2 tablespoons rosemary
1 tablespoon peppermint
20 drops bergamot oil
White washcloth
Hot bathwater

Add the lavender, rosemary, peppermint, and bergamot oil.

When temperature permits, submerge yourself. Take a few calming breaths and get into a peaceful state of mind. When ready, carefully wash yourself with the white washcloth. Begin at your head and go down to your feet. While washing, meditate on the change you are looking for. As you wash, you wash away the old and welcome the new.

After washing, spend at least 10 minutes relaxing in the water, meditating on the changes you are ushering into your life.

Water Elemental Bath

This is a purification bath for females.

2 tablespoons yarrow
2 tablespoons chamomile
20 drops ylang ylang oil
10 drops palmarosa oil
Steaming bathwater

Add the yarrow, chamomile, ylang ylang oil and palmarosa oil.

When temperature permits, submerge yourself and remain in the bath for at least 20 minutes. Spend this time concentrating on purifying yourself of anything negative you wish to get rid of. Visualize these things seeping through your skin and into the water.

When ready, exit the bath and drain the water. As you watch the water going down the drain, picture all negativity going with it. All that remains is purified and whole, and in you.

Earth Elemental Bath

This bath will help in gaining emotional stability.

20 drops patchouli oil
15 drops cypress oil
15 drops vertivert oil
Steaming bathwater

Add the patchouli, cypress, and vertivert oils.

When temperature permits, submerge yourself and remain in the bath for at least 20 minutes. While relaxing, visualize yourself standing on rock solid Earth. Whatever happens, the Earth will always be beneath your feet. Nothing can take away your support. Though you may stumble or fall, the Earth will always be there to catch you.

Fire Elemental Bath

This is a purification bath for males.

1 tablespoon basil
1 tablespoon juniper
20 drops frankincense oil
½ of a fresh orange
Red washcloth
Hot bathwater

Add the basil, juniper, and frankincense oil. The orange can be placed on the side of the tub.

When temperature permits, submerge yourself. Take a few calming breaths and get into a peaceful state of mind. When ready, take the orange half and squeeze it over your head. As the juice comes in contact with your body, imagine that it pulls out and traps any negativity affecting you.

Carefully wash yourself with the red washcloth. Begin at your head and go down to your feet. While washing, visualize yourself washing away any negativity. Once you are done washing, exit the bathtub and drain the negativity as quickly as possible.

General Wealth Attraction

This bath is used to attract wealth in a general way.

2 handfuls of parsley
Handful of rosemary
5 cinnamon sticks
Green bath salts
Hot bathwater

Add the parsley, rosemary, cinnamon sticks, and bath salts.

When temperature permits, submerge yourself. Take a few calming breaths to relax. When ready, visualize yourself in perfect financial harmony. You may see yourself shopping for goods, paying bills in full and on time, or receiving a paycheck. As long as you visualize you are in good financial health you are on the right path.

After at least 10 minutes, bathe yourself as you normally would.

To Attract Family Wealth

This bath is used to attract wealth towards your entire immediate family.

Handful of myrrh
2 lodestones
Olive oil
Green candle & carving tool
Green or golden washcloth
Olive oil based soap
Sunday
Warm bathwater

Begin this bathing ritual on a Sunday by drawing a warm bath.

Carve a dollar sign into the green candle and anoint it with olive oil.

Light the candle and place it anywhere in the bathroom which will allow you to bathe by candlelight.

Add the lodestones and myrrh to the bath water.

Submerge yourself for at least 10 minutes while focusing on great personal or family wealth. You can focus on either the family in general or you can focus on each family member individually, and imagine them as they would be financially successful.

When ready, bathe as you normally would. After bathing, pinch out the candle.

For the next 6 days, light the candle and bathe with the lodestones, allowing the candle to finish after the 7th bath.

Attract Money for a Specific Purpose

This bath is used to attract money for a specific purpose, usually a small amount.

2 lodestones
Small piece of quartz
Full moon
Warm bathwater

Place the lodestones in the bottom corners of the bathtub, near your feet. Place the crystal at the top of the bathtub, near your head.

In warm bathwater, bathe as you normally would. While bathing, concentrate on the specific thing you need money for. The lodestones and quartz should be kept in place for a full lunar cycle.

Getting a Job

This bath is used before a job interview to help you get mentally prepared and also bring a bit of luck your way.

Green or yellow bath salts, cinnamon scented
Handful of myrrh
Olive oil soap, green apple scented
Warm bathwater

The night before or morning of the interview, take this bath.

Add the bath salts and myrrh.

Submerge yourself and bath as you normally would, using the green apple soap. While bathing, focus on thinking about all the ways this particular job suits you and how exactly you would conduct yourself. This is also a good time to go over answers you feel you will be most likely to need during the interview.

When finished, dry yourself lightly while watching the bathwater drain away, taking any worries about this interview away from you.

Financial Turn it Around Bath

This bath should be used when you find yourself in a bad financial situation which you are looking to resolve.

Handful of parsley
1 cup goat's milk
1 stick cinnamon
Hot bathwater

Add the parsley, goat's milk, and cinnamon.

As temperature permits, submerge yourself and remain in the water until it cools down to room temperature. As the water cools, picture yourself going through the necessary steps to correct whatever financial problem you are currently working to resolve. Go step by step in your mind until you have a solid idea of what you need to do.

When the water is room temperature, exit the bath. This bath may be repeated every third night until the situation has been corrected.

Prize Winning Money Bath

This bath should be taken before any type of contest, no matter how big or small, in which the prize is money.

Tablespoon of brown sugar
Tablespoon of baking soda
Handful of parsley
Warm bathwater

This bath should be taken on the same day as the contest.

Add the brown sugar, baking soda, and parsley.

Submerge yourself and bathe as normal for at least 10 minutes.

You can repeat this bath as often as necessary for each contest you will be participating in.

Debt Banishing Bath

This bath is to banish debt, whether you are already in debt and want to shrink it or you are trying to keep from acquiring any debt.

4 ounces of baking soda
20 drops bergamot oil
Pinch of white sugar
Tall white candle
Warm bathwater

Add the baking soda and bergamot oil to warm bathwater and stir a few times with your dominant hand.

Break off the top of the white candle, discarding the broken piece over your right shoulder, and lighting the remainder. Place it anywhere in the bathroom which will allow you to bathe by candlelight. Once a bit of wax accumulates around the flame, sprinkle the sugar around the top of the candle to burn.

Enter and bathe as you normally would. When finished, discard the top candle piece out your back door.

This bath can be repeated once per lunar cycle as a defense against debt.

Good Business Bath

This bath should be taken if you need assistance with a particular business dealing. A good time to take this would be before an important meeting.

3 teaspoons of brown sugar
20 drops blue food coloring
Warm bathwater

Add the brown sugar and blue food coloring to a warm bath.

Bathe as normal and visualize your meeting, or any other specific activity related to your business. Picture everything happening as you would like to see it happening.

This bath may be used as often as necessary.

Business Bath for a Specific Need

This bath should be used to help raise money for something specific that you need in your business.

½ cup white sugar
20 drops of blue food coloring
Warm bathwater

Add the food coloring to warm water and stir counterclockwise with your left hand. Pour the sugar in the water and as you are pouring state your specific need out loud. Such as, "I need to raise money for an office computer." Don't talk an entire paragraph. State your need as simply as possible.

Submerge yourself and spend a few minutes concentrating on this object you are trying to draw. If it is something tangible (and it should be, for this bath) visualize holding it your hands or touching it. Then visualize yourself working as if you have already acquired your need.

This bath can be repeated weekly until your need has been met.

Couple's Bath

This bath is used to promote passion between couples in a romantic relationship.

Handful of fresh rosemary
Handful of dried lavender
Handful of dried yarrow
Handful of dried cardamom
Petals of a red rose
Rose scented soap (optional)
Steaming bathwater

Add the rosemary, lavender, yarrow, and cardamom to steaming bathwater. Add the rose petals last.

As temperature permits, enter the bath, woman first. Spend your time in the bath looking into each other's eyes, and making sure some part of your body is touching at all times. It is not necessary to talk. This bath works better in silence. The couple should wash each other, with rose scented soap if you have it. Normal soap is fine if allergies are an issue for either person.

When finished, dry off as normal. This bath can be taken by couples at any time.

Third Date Bath

This bath should be taken before a date if you are feeling particularly amorous. Despite the name, the number of dates you have been on is a nonissue.

5 oranges
Steaming bathwater

Cut 3 of the oranges in half, and squeeze them over steaming bathwater. The other oranges should be placed in the tub whole.

As temperature permits, submerge yourself. Soak for at least 20 minutes. Not only will you smell wonderful, but you will also feel better. Vitamin C (ascorbic acid) is absorbed by the skin, so you will get a physical boost before your hot date.

When finished bathing, rub the oranges across your body and then exit, allowing your body to air dry.

Looking for Love

This bath should be taken when you are looking to find a date.

Handful of parsley
5 cinnamon sticks
Petals of 3 red roses
Warm bathwater

Add the parsley, cinnamon sticks, and rose petals.

Submerge yourself and bathe as normal. This bath will make you look, feel, and smell more attractive while you go out and meet potential dates.

The parsley, cinnamon sticks, and rose petals should be thrown out your front door once the bathwater has finished draining.

Increase Sexual Energy

This bath can be taken to boost your sexual energy.

Ounce powdered Damiana leaf
Petals of a yellow rose
Handful of mint leaves
Quart of water
Warm bathwater

Add the Damiana leaf, rose petals, and mint leaves to a quart of water and bring to a boil. Allow approximately half of the mixture to boil off. Once cooled to room temperate, add everything to warm bathwater.

Submerge yourself and spend a few minutes just relaxing in the water. Once relaxed, you may choose an appropriate fantasy to get yourself more in the mood. When ready, bathe as normal.

This bath can be taken as often as necessary.

Strengthen a Romantic Relationship

This bath should be taken to add strength to a relationship that may have some weak spots.

Petals of 5 yellow roses
5 cinnamon sticks
5 teaspoons of honey
5 drops of your perfume
Yellow candle
Large bowl of water
Tuesday evening
Your preferred temperature bathwater

Add the rose petals, cinnamon sticks, honey, and perfume to the bowl of water and place it in a window that admits rays from the sunrise. If you must place the bowl outside in order to reach the sunrise, cover the bowl with cheesecloth.

At anytime on Wednesday after sunrise, add the contents of the bowl to your normal bath. Light the yellow candle and place it anywhere in the bathroom and bathe only by its light.

Submerge yourself and relax. Once relaxed, think of one thing in particular that your romantic partner does for you that you are grateful for. It is up to you whether you later express your gratefulness to your partner.

When finished, air dry, and pinch out the candle.

This bath should be repeated on consecutive Wednesdays for 5 weeks, using the same candle each week. On the 5th Wednesday, allow the candle to finish.

Romantic Dreams Bath

This bath is taken to help get your romantic life on your ideal path.

5 drops of attraction oil
10 drops of cinnamon oil
Teaspoon of honey
Teaspoon of vanilla extract
Cup of rose water
Hot bathwater

Add the ingredients to hot bathwater in the following order: honey, rose water, vanilla extract, cinnamon oil, and attraction oil. Stir the water with your left hand, counterclockwise.

Submerge and soak for at least half an hour, visualizing your romantic life as you want it to be for all of the future. Be as detailed as possible. Include dates, vacations, and an ideal sex life.

This bath can be taken weekly for as long as necessary.

Romantic Attraction Bath for Men

This bath is to be taken by men looking to attract a romantic partner.

Handful of sage
Handful of rosemary
Tablespoon of powdered vervain
Tablespoon of powdered vetivert
Tablespoon of powdered orris root
Teaspoon of powdered clover
Bay leaf
½ quart boiling water
Glass jar
Lukewarm bathwater

Boil all ingredients for 1 minute, and then reduce heat and simmer for 10 minutes.

Strain liquid into the glass jar.

Beginning on a Sunday, add about ½ cup (or approximately one seventh) from your jar to an evening bath.

Submerge yourself and soak for 10 minutes while visualizing all of the qualities you are looking for in a mate, as well as what you have to offer a mate. When finished visualizing, bathe as normal. Repeat this bath for 7 consecutive nights.

Romantic Attraction Bath for Women

This bath is to be taken by women looking to attract a romantic partner.

9 drops orange blossom oil
9 drops of sandalwood oil
9 drops clove oil
Nightfall
Warm bathwater

Add the orange blossom, sandalwood, and clove oil to a warm bath at nightfall.

Submerge yourself and say:

Water spirits please bring to me someone nice who cares. He will have a heart of gold, incapable of turning cold. He will be perfect to a tee, made just for me. As I will it, so mote it be.

Soak in the water for at least 15 minutes, visualizing yourself in a romantic relationship which is both what you desire, and what is right for you and the person you are with.

Repeat this bath for 7 consecutive nights.

Have Faith Bath

This bath should be taken to help you gain, maintain, or increase faith in your relationship.

Dried rose bud
5 cinnamon sticks
Ounce of powdered myrtle
Sprig of rosemary
Sprig of thyme
Teaspoon of honey
Lukewarm bathwater

Boil all ingredients for 1 minute, and then reduce heat and simmer for 10 minutes. Add the simmering mixture to lukewarm bathwater.

Submerge yourself and bathe as normal. While bathing, go over all the reasons you trust in and have faith in your partner and relationship. Think of only the positive things. Go over each in exact detail.

This bath can be taken as often as necessary.

Add a Spark to Love Bath

This bath should be taken to spark some fiery passion in your romantic life.

Sprig of thyme
Sprig of rosemary
1 tablespoon dried myrtle
5 drops musk oil
5 drops jasmine oil
Petals from a red rose
Acacia flower
Red washcloth
Steaming bathwater

Add the thyme, rosemary, myrtle, musk, and jasmine oils. The rose petals and acacia flower should be added when the water has cooled a bit and you are ready to begin the bath.

As temperature permits, submerge yourself. Bathe as normal while thinking over particularly passionate times you have spent with your partner in the past. Once in the right frame of mind, finish up and go to your partner.

This bath can be taken as often as you like.

Special Occasion Romance

This bath is to be taken before a special occasion you will spend with your partner such as an anniversary or birthday.

Handful of patchouli leaves
Handful of lemon verbena leaves
2 cinnamon sticks
5 drops vetivert oil
20 drops red food coloring
Steaming bathwater

Add the patchouli, lemon verbena, cinnamon sticks, and vetivert oil. Last add the red food coloring and stir a few times with your dominant hand. The goal is to have pink water.

As temperature permits, submerge yourself. Relax and visualize yourself, your partner, and all the positive accomplishments you have made up to this special occasion. Go over each accomplishment in detail.

Next visualize all the things you want to accomplish before the next special occasion, and picture yourself doing thing. After at least 20 minutes, bathe as normal to prepare for your celebratory evening and exit the bath.

Love Drawing Bath

This bath should be taken while you are preparing to see a person you would like to form a romantic relationship with.

Petals from a pink rose
Sprig of dill
½ cup anisette
Cool bathwater

Add the petals, dill, and last the anisette.

Submerge yourself and bathe as normal, spending at least 10 minutes in the bath. While bathing, speak out loud qualities you have that would benefit a romantic relationship. Be honest and don't exaggerate. This will send your intentions out in the world in a clear and concise way, helping your positive qualities be seen by the person you wish to attract.

Beautiful Body Bath

This bath should be taken to enhance your beauty.

2 geranium flowers
Red rose
Handful of rosemary
Warm bathwater

Add the geraniums, rose, and rosemary.

Submerge yourself and bathe as normal. This is a good time to use any beauty enhancing tools you have, such as a special hair conditioner or a facial mask. Focus on relaxing and loosening up.

This bath can be taking any time to keep you attractive.

Banish Negativity

This bath should be taken anytime you feel any sort of negativity.

8 ounces holy water
Petals of a white rose
¾ cup Epsom salt
White candle
Warm bathwater

Add the holy water, rose petals, and Epsom salt.

Light the white candle and place it anywhere it the bathroom so that you bathe only by its light.

Submerge yourself and bathe as normal for at least 20 minutes while concentrating on bringing peace of mind and repelling negativity. If you have a favorite prayer, this is the time to say it. You may pray or chant as long as you like while in the bath. When finished, pat yourself dry with a towel. The candle should be pinched out.

This bath can be taken as often as necessary.

Banish Soreness

This bath should be taken anytime your body feels sore or worn down in general.

1 cup sea water
1 teaspoon Epsom salt
Warm bathwater

Add the sea water and Epsom salt.

Submerge yourself in the bath for at least 15 minutes while, with eyes closed, you picture all physical soreness and discomfort flowing away from you. Bathe as normal.

When finished, drain the bath water and visualize all discomfort flowing down the drain away from you.

This bath can be taken as often as necessary.

Banish Anxiety

This bath should be taken anytime you need help getting rid of anxiety.

1 cup river water
1 cup Epsom salts
1 teaspoon baking soda
Yellow candle
Warm bathwater

Add the river water, Epsom salts, and baking soda. Light the candle, which should be placed on the edge of the bathtub near your feet. Bathe only by its light.

Submerge yourself for at least 20 minutes while visualizing the water forming a protective barrier around you. Take deep breaths and focus on releasing all anxiety within you. Because of the protective water barrier, no anxiety can get back in.

When finished, pinch out the candle and air dry. This bath can be taken as often as necessary.

Banish Sadness

This bath should be taken if you have felt a great sadness for an extended period of time and simply cannot recover from it.

1 tablespoon of powdered white eggshell
3 ounces of rose water
Petals from a white carnation
Warm bathwater

Add the powdered eggshell, rose water, and petals.

Submerge yourself for at least 15 minutes while visualizing the sadness seeping from your mind and body and into the water. When you have finished with that, next bathe as normal to further cleanse your body of any mental distress.

When finished, drain the bathtub. As the water is draining, visualize your sadness draining away with it. Pat yourself dry, collect the ingredients from the bathtub, and discard them far from your home. Discarding them at a crossroads is best.

This bath can be taken weekly.

Banish Anything

This basic banishing bath should be taken to banish anything you like.

1 cup goat's milk
Handful of parsley
1 teaspoon sea salt
Warm bathwater

Add the goat's milk, parsley, and sea salt.

Submerge yourself for at least 10 minutes while focusing all negative energy flowing away from you, and positive energy flowing toward you. Specifically focus on the thing you need to banish. Once it is visible to you, visualize your hand pushing it away from you. Continue to do this until you feel it is fully banished.

This bath can be taken once per lunar cycle.

Uncrossing Bath

This bath should be taken anytime you feel like someone is putting a hex on you, even a small one.

3 cups sea salt
Nighttime
Warm bathwater

Draw a hot bath, then allow the temperature to cool slightly.

Slowly pour the sea salt into the bath water, stirring it with your dominant hand. When the salt has dissolved, you may enter the water.

Say the following out loud three times:

I cast all evil far from me, as I will it, so mote it be!

Bathe as normal. This bath should be repeated for the next 6 consecutive nights.

Uncross Thoughts

This bath should be taken if another person is thinking and projecting negative thoughts towards you.

Clove of garlic
3 sage leaves
Pinch of dried basil
Handful of parsley
Bay Rum oil
Warm bathwater

Add the garlic, sage leaves, basil, and parsley to warm bathwater and allow them to soak for about 5 minutes.

Submerge yourself and take deep breaths until you feel calm and relaxed. Bathe as normal.

When finished, air dry, and then anoint your body with Bay Rum oil beginning at your shoulders and working towards your feet. As you rub the Bay Rum oil into your skin, say the following:

I am protected now with rum
No longer you harm me, your lips are mum
Any thought you think of me
Won't cause harm or negativity
So I will it, my will be done

Uncrossing any Hex

This bath should be taken if you feel a Hex upon you.

Christian Bible, *or* copies of Psalms 1 and 4, *or* memorize Psalms 1 and 4
Handful of powdered John the Conqueror's root
Warm bathwater

Outside the bathroom, speak out loud Psalm 1.

Enter the bathroom and draw a warm bath.

While the water is running, add the powdered John the Conqueror's root.

Submerge yourself in the bath for a maximum of 3 minutes.

Once out of the bathwater, recite Psalm 4 while air drying.

This bath can be taken daily.

Curse Removal Bath

This bath should be taken each day for 9 consecutive days to remove any curse on you.

2 tablespoons olive oil each day (amount may vary)

Take a bath as normal, be sure and scrub yourself extra clean. It is best to do this with as empty of a mind as you can manage.

When finished bathing, begin draining the water and stand up in the tub.

Anoint your body with olive oil, beginning at the shoulders and moving down. When finished, pat yourself dry.

Continue this ritual for a total of 9 days.

On the 9th day go through the ritual as before, and then collect a cupful of bath water. The cup of bathwater should be taken outside and flung towards the sun to finish the ritual.

Uncross Evil

This bath should be taken to thwart evil.

3 drops camphor oil
3 drops eucalyptus oil
Splash of your own urine (optional)
Early morning
Your preferred temperature bathwater

This must be the first thing of the day that you do.

Add the camphor and eucalyptus oils and splash of urine to the water. It is fine to add the urine directly from its source.

Bathe as normal.

When finished, while you are draining the water, visualize the water washing away with it all manner of jinxes, hexes, or curses which may be affecting you.

Pat yourself dry with a towel.

This bath can be repeated daily if necessary.

Uncross Negative Energy

This bath should be taken to remove negative energy

Ounce of bloodroot powder
Cup of sea salt
Cup of Epsom salt
Lukewarm bathwater

Add all ingredients to lukewarm bath water and stir a few times with your dominant hand.

Submerge yourself and soak for at least 20 minutes. Allow any negativity to seep from your body and into the bath water. Visualize negativity (usually easily visualized as black or gray) seeping out of your skin and into the water, where it becomes diluted.

When finished, drain the water while visualizing all negativity flowing away from you, and allow yourself to air dry.

This bath may be repeated weekly.

Basic Luck Bath

This bath should be taken for a general increase in luck.

Tablespoon of powdered cinnamon
Long stemmed red rose
Sprig of parsley
Vase
Blue food coloring
Morning
Warm bathwater

Begin by drawing the bath. Fill your vase with water, add 2 drops of blue food coloring and swish to combine. Set the vase in the center of your home.

To warm bathwater, add the cinnamon and parsley.

Bathe as normal, focusing on surrounding yourself with only good luck as you do.

When finished, air dry.

The rose should be placed in the vase of blue water at the center of your home and cared for. When adding water in the future, it is not necessary to dye it blue. When the rose dies, your luck is reduced to the level it was before you took this bath. Discard the rose out your front door and you may begin again.

Good Luck While Travelling

This bath should be taken before travelling.

Christian Bible, *or* a copy of Psalm 23, *or* memorize Psalm 23
Ounce of alfalfa
Ounce of dried chamomile flowers
5 cinnamon sticks
Silverweed leaf
Bay leaf
Sprig of rosemary
Boiled water
Sunday
Warm bathwater

This bath will be taken for 7 consecutive days and should begin on a Sunday. This ritual should be completed before you begin travelling, so plan accordingly.

Add everything to boiled water and allow it to steep for 7 minutes.

After steeping, strain, and then add to warm bathwater. Keep the pot handy.

Submerge yourself in the water. With your pot, pour bath water of the top of your head 7 times. While you are doing this, speak Psalm 23.

When finished, pat yourself dry with a towel.

This bath should be repeated every day for 7 days.

Healthy and Wealthy with Luck

This bath should be taken for luck with health, wealth, or both.

Cup of holy water
Pot of water
Bay leaf
Sprig of Rosemary
Hot bathwater

Boil the bay leaf and rosemary for 1 minute.

Add first the boiled water (including the rosemary and bay), and then the holy water, to your bath. As you are pouring the holy water say:

House of Jerusalem, where Christ was born, clear my soul of any sin, only allowing goodness within.

Submerge yourself in the bath and say:

Cleanse my soul, rosemary, and fill my bowl with gold. Health and wealth protected by bay, this I say.

Remain in the water for at least 15 minutes. Visualize yourself as you want to be.

This bath can be repeated weekly.

Lucky Winner

This bath should be taken for luck winning prizes or contests, the lottery included.

5 oranges
7 strawberries
7 green grapes
Warm bathwater

Add the oranges, strawberries, and grapes.

Enter the bath, and run each fruit across your body.

Remain in the water for at least 20 minutes. You should visualize yourself winning the contest or prize. If it's a Bingo game, picture yourself filling your Bingo card and accepting your prize. If it's a door prize, visualize your name being drawn and read out in front of all your friends. Be careful to visualize as accurately as possible.

When finished, air dry. The fruits should be flung as far possible out your back door.

This bath can be taken as often as necessary.

Daily Luck Ritual

This bath can be taken each day for a small boost to your luck.

Handful of dried rosemary
Handful of dried bay leaves
Handful of dried violet flowers
Handful of dried silverweed
Glass jar
Your preferred temperature bathwater

Combine all ingredients in a glass jar and shake. Keep the jar in your bathroom.

Sprinkle some of these herbs in your normal bathwater at the beginning of the day.

Submerge yourself, bathe, and dry off as normal.

This can be done regularly for general luck.

Made in the USA
Lexington, KY
08 May 2014